From Passion to Profit

MONETIZE THE THINGS YOU LOVE AND LOVE TO DO

A GUIDE FOR YOUTH AND YOUNG ADULTS

Jeffrey Ulysse, M.S.Ed.

PUBLISHING

Images from 123rf.com
Editing and typesetting by Sally Hanan of Ink-snatcher.com
Cover design by Chris Descartes of Rocket Science Creative Labs

Ordering Information: Quantity sales. Special discounts are available on quantity purchases by corporations, associations, and others. For details,

info@juconsultants.com

From Passion to Profit/Jeffrey Ulysse. —1st ed.

ISBN 978-1-7331454-0-4

To my grandfather Estera Ulysse. As you rest in power, your memory, your convictions, and your love live on through me.

Contents

Introduction

A Call for Deployment

Introduction
A Call for Deployment

Nelson Mandela once said,

"There is no passion to be found playing small—in settling for a life that is less than the one you are capable of living."

I've discovered that our culture has conditioned our youth and young adults to play small, to settle for a life that's less than the one they are truly capable of living. Our culture conditions our young people to forfeit their dreams in exchange for economic fulfillment, thereby sacrificing self-actualization rather than achieving personal fulfillment.

I am a learned, educated man with several degrees and an avid supporter and believer in education. I believe the pristine standard and purpose of education is two-fold: draw and bring forth. I believe that education is designed to draw out the gifts in you, to bring forth the passion in you in such a manner that it would cause you to recognize the value on the inside of you! This causes you to be knowledgeable, profitable, and trans-actional in the marketplace of the world.

But sadly, for some this hasn't been the case. Our own educational system has damaged them and caused them to settle for a life that says, "Go to school, get a degree, get a job"—and then waste away in retirement. This system places too much of an emphasis on preparing our young people for employment.

In 2017, the *Huffington Post* updated a mind-blowing article which stated, "There are 900 million people in 142 countries who are unfulfilled with what they do in life. In the U.S. alone, 70 percent of people working are unhappy and don't care for what they do." If that isn't alarming enough, the article goes on to mention that "Millennials are the most unfulfilled and care least about what they do at work. . . . the majority of the 79 million U.S Millennials are either unemployed, underpaid, or weighed down with student loans."[1]

With this fresh in mind, and considering our current social and economic conditions in our world, now more than ever we must prime our young people and ready them for deployment!

Now is the time in which you must learn to discover the source of your value, which is hidden in your gift.

Now is the time you must learn how to liquidate your passions and seek ways to monetize the things you love and love to do!

Now is the time you must go on to do not just what you have been created to do but have been packaged and deployed to do!

This book is intended to cause a generation of youth, young adults, and Millennials to venture out on an introspective journey of self-discovery that would result in the realization that

You can, in fact, create the life you imagine for yourself. I implore you and remind you once more of the words of Nelson Mandela: "There is no passion to be found playing small—in settling for a life that is less than the one you are capable of living."!

Jeffrey Ulysse, M.S.Ed.

Notes

[1] Bratasanu, D. (2017, January 7). "900 Million People in the World Are Unfilled with Their Work. Here's What To Do If You're One of Them." *Www.huffpost.com*. Retrieved from https://www.huffpost.com/entry/900-million-people-in-the_b_8917818.

Passion

Seeing the Beginning and the End

CHAPTER 1

Passion
Seeing the Beginning and the End

Passion is having a sense of strong arduous love and emotion for a thing. The word *passion* comes from the Latin word "passio," which refers to suffering. When one is passionate of a thing, they are suffered or subjected to the thing whereas they are completely overcome and undone with the burning feeling of desire for the thing that consumes them.

To be passionate is to be suffered, and the word *suffer* speaks of a bearing, that is, a carrying. To be passionate is to be carrying. Passion is meant to cause you to be fertile, it is meant to cause you to reproduce, giving birth to that which has subjected and consumed you.

Passion is, simply put, the ability to give life to that which has impregnated you, to endure the suffering of labor pains and push out that idea, invention, business, or dream that you can't stop thinking about, the one that literally keeps you up at night and wakes you up in the morning.

I offer to you that your passion desires to bring about a world and a future that is on the inside of you.

Your passion enables you to see the end of the thing so that you would birth the beginning of the thing.

Passion provides you with the fuel to work toward the destination of completion. In addition, your passion can also be likened to and utilized as a compass. It's designed to help you identify and locate your gift, leading you to a place of personal fulfillment and achieving the pinnacle of Maslow's hierarchy: self-actualization.

So the big ask is this:

> **What are you passionate about?**
>
> **What moves you?**
>
> **What end do you see so that you would begin to birth its beginnings?**

I offer to you that you can monetize your loves, not your likes. I offer to you that you can create the life and the world you imagine for yourself. I offer to you that you can take your passion, package it, and turn it into a product that will yield you a profit, irrespective of your age, race, gender, or class rules.

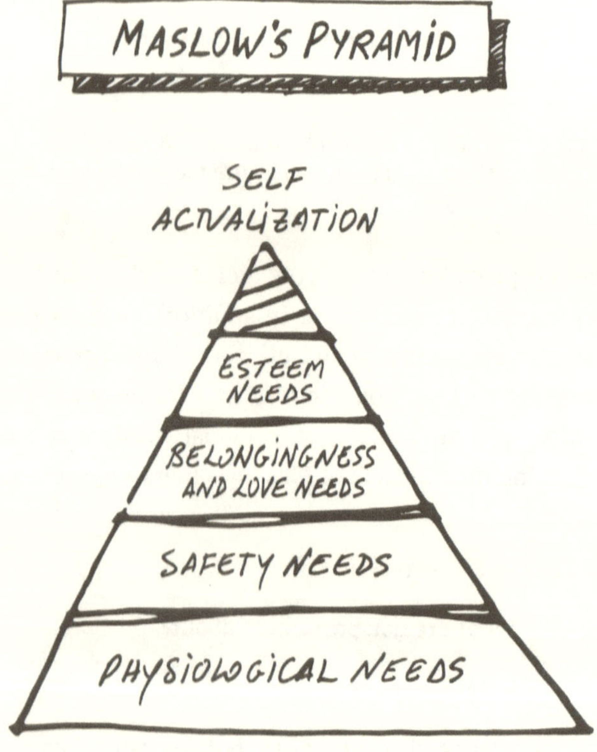

Activity

Passion Finder

ACTIVITY

PASSION FINDER

THE PURPOSE OF THIS PASSION FINDER EXERCISE IS TO STIMULATE YOUR THINKING SO THAT TOGETHER WE CAN LOCATE YOUR PASSION.

List five hobbies or niches you enjoy doing. Identify and circle if each hobby is a _like_ or a _love_.

____

love or like

____

love or like

____

love or like

____

love or like

____

love or like

Which hobby, interest, or activity, when in motion, makes you feel timeless (as if you've lost track of time)?

____

____

____

____

____

____

What are your favorite subjects in school?

____

____

____

____

____

____

What subject do you perform the absolute best in, and your grades show the result?

____

List five strengths and five weaknesses.

Strengths	Weakness

What do you feel brings you the greatest joy or satisfaction and makes you light up inside?

____

____

____

____

____

____

If there were one breakdown (problem) in the world that you could solve, what would it be? Why do you feel connected to that issue?

____

____

____

____

____

If you could get a public service announcement to a massive amount of people, what would your message be?

____

____

____

____

____

If you had the power to create anything you wanted or bring to life any idea, invention, cure, project, or business, what would it be? Why did you choose it?

____

____

____

____

____

If you had financial stability and flexibility, what could you see yourself doing for the rest of your life?

____

____

____

____

____

After completing this exercise and reviewing your responses, what do you feel you are passionate about?

____

____

____

____

Gifts

The Midas Touch

CHAPTER 2

Gifts
The Midas Touch

A gift or talent is defined as an innate, intrinsic ability that cannot be learned, only cultivated and nurtured. In other words, a gift is something you use naturally and effortlessly well. When in operation, its results are undeniable, and it often feels like you've got the Midas touch—everything you set your hands to is so successful it turns to gold!

When we're in a conversation about talents, we often make the major mistake of glorifying and placing more of an emphasis on abilities such as being able to sing, dance, or play a musical instrument, as if that's the barometer for having a viable gift! Sadly, as a result,

Too many young people overlook their abilities because they're too focused on trying to fit themselves into a box of performance.

I'm here to let you know it is okay to not be able to sing, dance, or play an instrument. Those are not the only abilities we've been given.

If you are a great communicator or orator, you have a gift.

If you're really great at serving and providing for those in need with aid and support, you have a gift.

If you have a knack for teaching, imparting knowledge, and disseminating information, you have a gift.

If you're a natural at providing encouragement and inspiration, you have a gift!

If you tend to assume leadership positions and are a positive role model to others, you have a gift!

If understanding the sciences of health and medicine comes to you effortlessly, you have a gift.

If you're an excellent writer, you have a gift.

If you're amazing at doing hair, nails, and makeup, you have a gift.

If you have an eye for fashion, colors, prints, and patterns, you have a gift.

If you're really good with children and they flock to you, you have a gift.

If you seem to understand the needs and language of babies, you have a gift.

If you have the ability to draw and paint, and you're incredibly artistic, you have a gift.

If nobody cooks and bakes like you and you've gotten nonstop reviews and recommendations, you have a gift.

If you're great at fixing things and solving problems and you think critically, you have a gift.

If you're great with technology and understand how electrical appliances work, you have a gift.

If you're great at creating and building things and creating architectural drawings, you have a gift.

I say this to show you that whatever you can do better than most others, and it comes effortlessly to you, that indeed is a gift you have. I encourage you to hone in on these skills and really take the time to develop them.

I often wonder what would happen if we stopped looking outwardly and started looking inwardly? What if we decided to stop looking at what other people have and focus instead on what we have inside us? Take the time to tap in and invest in your gift!

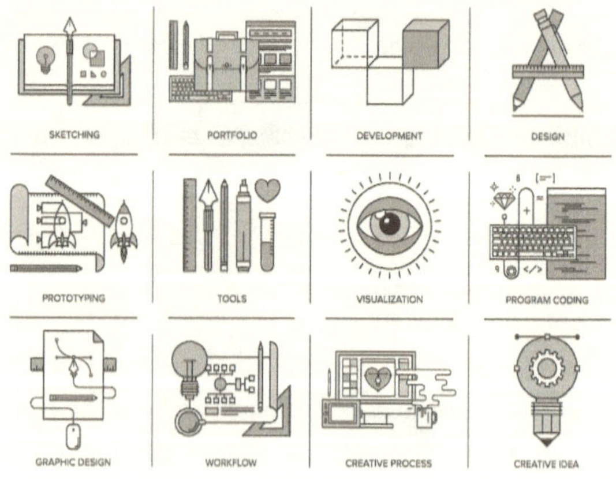

Activity

Hard Skills and Soft Skills

ACTIVITY

HARD SKILLS AND SOFT SKILLS

In the previous chapter, I mentioned that another word for *gift* can be "talent" or "ability." In essence, we're in a conversation about skills, skill sets, and finding your place. It's important to understand the lexicon of the marketplace of the world. What exactly is it looking for? It's looking for the value you have to offer.

Your value is found in your gift.

For you to transact effectively with the world's marketplace, you must be able to not only identify your abilities but understand which are hard skills and which are soft skills.

What exactly are hard skills and soft skills? Hard skills are more technical abilities that are tangible and able to be quantifiable (expressed and measured). They are sets of skills apprehended through experience, education, or training. A few examples of some hard skills are computer expertise, reading competence, writing ability, foreign language proficiency, math aptitude, and coding and programming skills.

Soft skills are referred to as *people skills* or *interpersonal skills*. These abilities are intangible and unquantifiable (difficult to measure) and demonstrate how you interact with other people. Some examples of soft skills are adeptness in communication, leadership skills, teamwork abilities, creativity, time management, critical thinking, and adaptability.

The debate in educational circles is about what skills are highly necessary for success. I believe a mixture of hard skills and soft skills is the main ingredient for the meal of success. You need the balance and integration of people/interpersonal skills (soft) and technical skills/tangible abilities (hard) to create your world.

Hard Skills (technical/tangible abilities)	Soft Skills (people/interpersonal skills)
Computer skills – coding/programming	Communication and leadership
Reading/writing	Creativity
Foreign language	Time management and organization
Artistic ability	Critical thinking
Math	Teamwork

Let me provide you with a modern example of hard and soft skills. Cardi B., for example, has a hard, or technical, skill of knowing how to rap. Cardi's soft skills—that is, her people skills—are her creativity, savviness, and likability.

What do you think your hard skills are?

____

____

____

____

____

What do you think your soft skills are?

____

____

____

____

____

Remember, the marketplace is looking for what you have to offer. If you can locate your abilities, I offer to you that you can find your place in the world to not just be profitable but to be purposeful and impactful.

Gifts + Passion

The Harmonious Union

CHAPTER 3

Gifts + Passion
The Harmonious Union

Your gift and passion are not to be separable or divisible; in fact, they should be a cohesive force, tightly weaved together like a three-strand cord, which is certainly difficult to break. There is intended to be a harmonious relationship between the gift (natural unlearned ability) and passion (suffered with an ardent feeling of love and desire).

Consider this illustration to help provide you with a greater understanding and context. If I were to light an object on fire, immediately that object would then emit smoke. The fumes are a result of that which has been set ablaze. In this illustration, the object refers to the gift, and the fumes refer to your passion. Your passions are the fumes of fervent love and desire that come from your gift and natural ability!

The union between your gift and passion gives you the ability to conceive twins named Purpose and Vision. It births purpose in you, revealing to you your aims, and answers the question why. It creates vision in you, offering you portraits of purpose and giving you the ability to see to conceive.

Conception only comes through the birth canal of imagination!

I encourage you to take some time and invest in yourself. You will be surprised of what you're truly capable of. The world is watching and waiting for you to rise in the innocence of a dove and strike in the shrewdness of a serpent.

It is absolutely integral that the fires of passion do not die out. Surround yourself with like-minded people who would serve as combustibles to feed and fan the flame of your passion and encourage you to cultivate the talents you've been given.

Now let me ask you,

What are you hoarding?

What are you sitting on?

What are you burying?

Have you not realized what's in you?

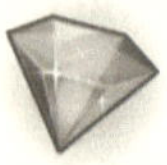

I want you to know this truth: what you don't realize, you will never materialize, and what you do not materialize, you cannot monetize!).

Activity

Making "Cents"

ACTIVITY

MAKING "CENTS"

IN THIS EXERCISE, WE'RE GOING TO BRING THIS ALL TOGETHER WHERE IT ALL MAKES "CENTS." FIRST, I'D LIKE TO USE MYSELF AS AN EXAMPLE TO HELP GUIDE YOU THROUGH THIS ACTIVITY.

What are you passionate about?

I am passionate about youth development; I have a fervid love for youth and young adults.

What is your gift?

I am gifted in my ability to use my language and words to encourage and inspire.

What does the relationship between your gift and passion look like?

I use my gift to motivate and encourage youth and young adults, whom I have an intense love for.

How can the union between your gift and passion produce monetization or monetary results?

My passion (love) served as a compass that led me to explore careers around serving young people. My gift, or my niche, showed me my fit. As a result, I've found success as a youth empowerment speaker and motivator.

BONUS QUESTIONS

Can you identify your soft skill?

My soft skill is my communication skills.

Can you identify your hard skill?

My hard skill is my proficiency in reading and writing that provides me with the skills to produce language.

OKAY, SO NOW IT'S YOUR TURN! I WANT YOU TO BE FOCUSED AND INTENTIONAL.

Ready, set, go for it...

What are you passionate about?

____

____

____

____

____

____

____

What is your gift?

____

____

____

____

____

What does the relationship between your gift and passion look like?

____

____

____

____

____

____

How can the union between your gift and passion produce monetary results for you?

____

____

____

____

____

____

BONUS QUESTIONS

Can you identify your soft skill?

____

____

Can you identify your hard skill?

____

____

Value

The Marketplace's Eyes on You

CHAPTER 4

Value
The Marketplace's Eyes on You

Value is determined and measured by *significance, desirability, worth,* and *usefulness.* The ability must carry the weight of significance and importance. The gift must bear meaning and be consequential—that is, it must have a relationship between positive cause and effect that can create change. Does your natural talent have the capability to serve as the cause or catalyst that can influence change?

I previously mentioned that the source of your value is hidden in your gift. Additionally,

The source of your wealth is found in the gift— that which brings you value!

You have to measure your value and ask yourself,

Is what I have in me worthy of wanting?

Is it attractive?

Does it arouse desire?

Finally, is there a demand in the marketplace of the world for what I have to offer?

Attached to the gift must be the measure of worth. It must be clothed in the quality and costly fabric of excellence. Does it have the potential to command esteem, attention, and money? You must understand that money is attracted to value. The more you increase in value, the more you whet the appetite of money and turn its eyes toward you because it has a taste for you. We must get into a practice of not trying to chase and pursue money.

Quite frankly, chasing money is like chasing the wind, like you're fighting against the air current in a cash-grab machine.

So find ways to increase your value, and ask yourself,

Does this ability that I have in me carry worth?

The truth of the matter is that your worth is tied to your net worth.

Finally, value is measured by usefulness. Ask yourself,

Is this ability capable of serving some purpose?

Is it helpful?

Can this gift produce real results and supply need in a market of demand?

Is it able to be used advantageously and for the benefit of others?

I want you to understand this truth: the marketplace of the world is not looking *for you* but for *what's in you*! The marketplace is asking these questions: What can you do? What do you have to offer? If you can answer these questions, then you've found your place in the world. Get ready to take your seat among the legends after you've done the work! This is how value is determined and measured. This is the lens in which you must critically view and judge your talent.

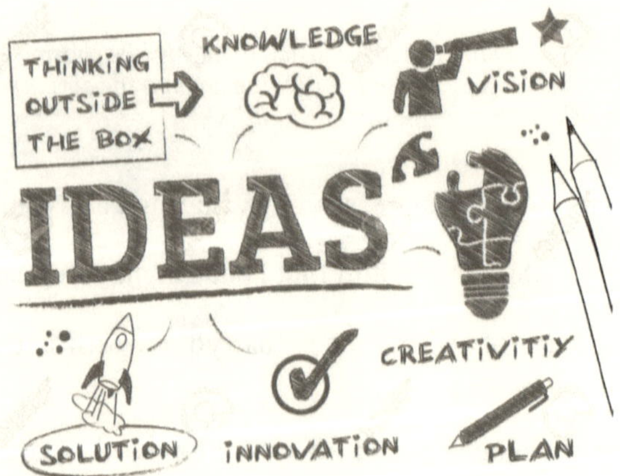

Activity

Measuring Your Value

ACTIVITY

MEASURING YOUR VALUE

SIGNIFICANCE PROMPT

Do you feel that your abilities carry the weight of significance and importance? Does your gift have a relationship between creating positive cause and effect (i.e., change)?

Part A. What are your abilities, and what significance do you feel they bear?

____

____

____

____

____

Part B. How might your abilities be used in creating change?

____

____

____

____

____

DESIRABILITY PROMPT

Is the ability you have to offer worthy of wanting? Do you think it can arouse desire? Is there a demand in the marketplace for that which you are the supply of?

Part A: Can you identify and make any connections to markets, fields, or careers that your abilities are related to or can be used in? What are they?

____

____

____

____

____

____

Part B: Can you articulate this in language and share your "why"? Provide a statement of justification that supports your claim in one sentence.

____

____

____

____

____

____

WORTH PROMPT

Do your abilities have the potential to command esteem, attention, and money?

Part A: Can you identify one way you can take your ability and turn it into a product that can be packaged and pitched?

____

____

____

____

____

____

Part B: If you could put a monetary price tag on the value of your ability (product) that you would package and pitch, what would it be worth?

$_____________

USEFULNESS PROMPT

Is your ability capable of serving some purpose? Is it helpful? Can this gift produce real results? Is it able to be used advantageously and for the benefit of others?

Part A: Can you identify a potential or legitimate need in the world for what you have to offer?

____

____

____

____

____

____

Part B: What breakdown (problem) can your abilities be the breakthrough (solution) for?

____

____

____

____

____

____

Clarity

Cases of Monetization

CHAPTER 5

Clarity
Cases of Monetization

The "Sweet" Story of Mikaila Ulmer

Mikaila Ulmer is the CEO and founder of BeeSweet Lemonade (now Me & the Bees Lemonade). This young girl appeared on *Shark Tank* around the age of nine, ready to pitch a "sweet" deal. Mikaila immediately let the sharks know her product was unique and vastly different from many other lemonades out there. She talked about how her product was beneficial for one's health and tastier than what was on the market. She clearly communicated her design ideas and the purpose of her lemonade company.

To Mikaila, it wasn't just about selling lemonade—she wanted to make a measurable impact on saving the bee population. Mikaila's ability to identify a breakdown in our world and offer a breakthrough was something I thought was simply masterful.

I believe this focus and intention led her to secure a deal with the sharks. Interestingly, at the time she was on *Shark Tank* it was noted that her lemonade was in thirty-five stores. After *Shark Tank*, her brand is now in over two hundred stores in the United States. She is in partnership with Marquee Brands, and others are interested in her product. More recently, Mikaila landed an $11 million distribution deal with Whole Foods.

During a recap of the show, one of the sharks asked Mikaila what her greatest challenge was with running her lemonade company. She responded by saying that the challenge she was experiencing was fitting school, BeeSweet Lemonade, and all her extracurricular activities into her schedule. What I find amazing about this is that she balances her business all while making straight As in school. In addition, she makes time to deliver personal sales pitches in grocery stores.

This brilliant young girl demonstrates exceptional communication skills, time management, and flexibility, and she has specialized knowledge about the bee population—not to mention she's great in sales and marketing. Mikaila is just another example of a person, regardless of age, taking her passion, packaging it, and turning it into a product that's yielding her a "sweet" profit!

The Story of a Business That's "BOOMIN"

Meet Benjamin Kapelushnik or "Kickz," teenage sneaker mogul who is also known as the "Sneaker Don." Ben's love for sneakers has led him to launch his very own self-made sneaker resell business where he purchases and "flips" sneakers.

I watched a video of Ben in which he shared how it all began. He started selling sneakers to his friends and classmates when he was in the fourth grade. His parents didn't want to fund a "hobby," so he had to start by reselling the sneaker collection he already had to fund what really wasn't a hobby but a passion.

Ben realized what he was doing had the potential to become a legitimate business when all the kids at school wanted his shoes. Ben was so savvy that he would pay people to wait in lines to get the latest, hottest, and in-demand sneakers.

It's pretty amazing how the "Sneaker Don" never really intended to make a business out of his passion. Later on, he saw the capacity for a huge earning potential. Ben used his ingenuity by buying sneakers in bulk and reselling them on his very own website.

Ben has a celebrity clientele featuring a number of high-profile rappers and athletes who go to him for rare sneakers before they are released to the public. He's known for his video that went viral with DJ Khalid. Khalid asked Ben, "How's business?" Ben responded, "Boomin."

Ben's tact approach and use of his social media and branding and marketing is absolutely amazing and remarkable. He is bringing in massive returns on the investments he's made. Ben is just another young person who has gone from passion to profit.

The Stylish Story of Mo's Bows

Meet Moziah Bridges, CEO of Mo's Bows. I first encountered this young man's story when I watched him present his business proposal to the sharks on *Shark Tank*. At the time, the young man was about eleven years old when he had his pitch presentation. As I watched Mo, I was immediately drawn in by his natural charm and his ability to clearly articulate the story behind Mo's Bows with such style and swag.

Mo mentioned how he always loved to look dapper. He talked about when he was younger, he would go to the playground and dress up in a suit and tie. He mentioned how hard it was for him to find a tie that he liked, so his grandmother taught him how to sew. As soon as he learned how to sew, he launched Mo's Bows and began creating bow ties that he fell in love with. Mo would then go on and give people advice that they should "figure out what they like to do" and "find out how to make money from it"!

Mo clearly was keen on how to turn his passion into profit. What I appreciated more about his presentation was that Mo wasn't just *clear* on his why but he exuded *confidence* in his why. Mo's chief aim and purpose is to help people look good so they will feel good. That is exactly what Mo has done and continues to do. He's gone from a young man who struck a deal on *Shark Tank* at eleven years old to a teenager with an internationally recognized brand that continues to yield tremendous results. Mo recently landed a deal with the National Basketball Association. NBA fans now have a fun, creative, and stylish way to support their favorite teams by wearing his Mo's Bows NBA collection!

What's the Point?

It was my intent and desire that you would not only be inspired from the stories of Mikaila, Benjamin, and Mo but that you would find the motivation to grab a shovel, start digging, and put some action behind your passion. You too, just like these three amazing young individuals, can, in fact, turn your passion into profit.

I want you to understand that your riches are in your niches. There's passion in you that's designed to pay you.

I hope that these cases will help you recognize the creative power inside of you and that you would come into relationship with the passion, natural ability, and endowments that have made their abode in you. I am certain something great dwells inside you that has value, meets a need, and has some serious earning capacity and potential that will leave the marketplace of the world salivating on your behalf!

Activity

Case of Monetization Quiz

ACTIVITY

CASE OF MONETIZATION QUIZ

IN THE CASE STUDIES WE JUST EXAMINED, LET'S SEE IF YOU ARE ABLE TO IDENTIFY THE FOLLOWING. IF YOU CAN CLEARLY SEE IT IN SOMEONE ELSE, THEN THAT MEANS WE ARE ON THE ROAD TO SELF-DISCOVERY, AND ONE STEP CLOSER TO GOING FROM PASSION TO PROFIT.

IN THE SWEET STORY OF MIKAILA ULMER . . .

What is Mikaila's passion?

What is Mikaila's gift?

How has Mikaila turned her passion into profit?

What do you think are Mikaila's soft skills?

____

____

____

____

____

____

What do you think are Mikaila's hard skills?

____

____

____

____

____

____

In measuring Mikaila's value, what is the significance of her lemonade?

____

____

____

____

____

____

Is there desirability?

____

____

____

____

____

____

Is worth present?

____

____

____

____

____

How is it useful?

____

____

____

____

____

IN THE STORY OF A BUSINESS THAT'S BOOMIN . . .

What is Benjamin's passion?

____

____

____

What is Benjamin's gift?

____

____

____

____

How has Benjamin turned his passion into profit?

____

____

____

____

What do you think are Benjamin's soft skills?

____

____

____

____

____

What do you think are Benjamin's hard skills?

____

____

____

____

____

In measuring Benjamin's value, what is the significance of his sneaker company?

____

____

____

____

____

Is there desirability?

____

____

____

____

____

Is worth present?

____

____

____

____

____

How is it useful?

____

____

IN THE STYLISH STORY OF MO'S BOWS, CAN YOU IDENTIFY THE FOLLOWING?

What is Mo's passion?

What do you think is Mo's gift?

How has Mo turned his passion into profit?

What do you think are Mo's soft skills?

What do you think are Mo's hard skills?

____

____

____

____

____

In measuring Mo's value, what is the significance of his bows?

____

____

____

____

____

Is there desirability?

____

____

____

____

____

Is worth present?

____

____

____

____

____

____

How is it useful?

____

____

____

____

____

____

Habits

Habits Form Future

CHAPTER 6

Habits
Habits Form Future

A habit is a practice, a consistent way of being. It is your consistent practice that comes from your way of being that becomes involuntary. I have discovered something quite powerful about habits. Habits are formative. For example, an infant or young child who makes a practice out of sucking their thumb literally can cause changes in the roof of their mouth. In addition, if you make a consistent practice out of going to the gym, you are forming your body structure. In like manner, habits form futures.

The difference between successful people and unsuccessful people is not only in ability and education but also in their habits. Much literature can be found on this topic. One of the most popular books—which you've probably heard of—is *The Seven Habits of Highly Effective People*. Let me tell you something:

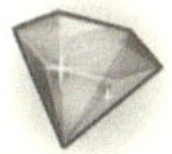 *Success and failure are both designed to be predictable!*

The funny thing about habits is they can serve as a self-predicting prophecy. I don't have to be a fortuneteller to see where you'll end up—I'm certain your habits will reveal your future.

I encourage you to make a practice out of developing and cultivating your abilities and take the time to create spaces for mindfulness, meditation, and self-exploration. Remember, the source of your value is hidden in your gift, and the source of your wealth is found in the gift!

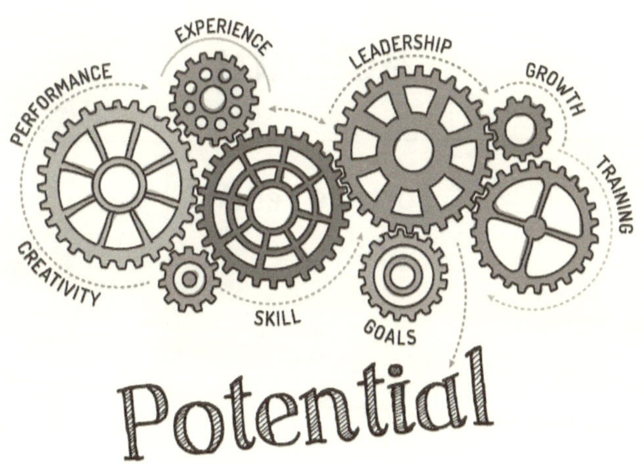

Activity

Fortune Teller

ACTIVITY

FORTUNE TELLER

IN THIS ACTIVITY, OUR GOAL IS TO CREATE AWARENESS, AND AWARENESS IS VITAL TO CREATING CHANGE. WE'RE GOING TO TAKE A LOOK AT SOME NEGATIVE HABITS THAT HAVE THE POTENTIAL TO FORM FAILURE AND POSITIVE HABITS THAT HAVE THE POTENTIAL TO FORM SUCCESS.

What are at least three negative habits I currently practice?

How will I end my relationship with these practices?

Note: Your plan should be practical. Something that is practical is fit for practice. It is ready for action and application.

What are at least three positive habits I currently practice?

____

____

____

What are at least three positive habits I would like to practice?

____

____

____

Plans

The Transition

CHAPTER 7

Plans
The Transition

You've decided to respond to the call and challenge of deployment! You've made up your mind to journey with me. Our ultimate goal was to transition from passion to profit, and now we have reached the very moment!

Thus far, you've identified your passion, located your gift, and discovered your hard and soft skills. You've thought through the relationship between your gift and your passion, measured your value, studied cases of monetization, and shared how your habits are vital to your success.

Now you're ready to go from passion to profit; you're ready to take your passion, package it, and turn it into a product that will create a stream of revenue for you. Earlier, in the exercise Making Cents, I talked about how the union between your gift and your passion might produce monetary results. The purpose of that exercise was to draw and lead you to the place of identifying the product, goods, or services you can offer the marketplace.

I hope you've discovered what that particular product, good, or service is because now you are going to create a business plan. This is how you legitimately transition from passion to profit. Every business needs a plan. Yours will be the foundation, guide, and tool that helps you operate your business. It is absolutely vital to your success and serves two purposes:

- to provide direction

- to attract investors who will fund or raise capital for your business

There are essentially two types of business plans—the traditional plan, which encourages you to be detailed and thorough in your description, and the lean start-up plan, which helps you summarize the major or core components of your plan.

The Traditional Business Plan

It's time to make some magic and focus your energy on the more traditional business plan.

"There is no magic in magic. It's all in the details."
— Walt Disney

The U.S. Small Business Administration recommends that a traditional business plan include some combination of the following: executive summary, company description, market analysis, organization and management structure, service or product description, marketing and sales strategy, and funding request.[1]

EXECUTIVE SUMMARY

Your summary should explain what your business is all about. In it you can provide your mission statement and concisely talk about your product, your team (if you chose to have one), and your desired location.

An executive summary is a picture of your business. It should capture your why, as your why is the key to your drive. If you have no why, you will have no drive, and you'll watch as life passes you by.

COMPANY DESCRIPTION

The company description describes exactly what it is that you do. This is where you show that what your business or product offers is the breakthrough people have been looking for or the solution to a problem. In addition, you want to name your desired target audience, how you plan to meet their needs, and what distinguishes you from the rest of the pack in your related industry.

MARKET ANALYSIS

Market analysis is where you roll up your sleeves, strap on your boots, and get ready to do the real work—research. In your market analysis, you want to know who your competitors are, what their strengths and weakness are, and any similar patterns, trends, or themes that stand out. You've got to be able to answer these questions to distinguish yourself from the competition. You've got the supply; now you must do your research carefully so you can assess and meet the need and exceed demand.

ORGANIZATION AND MANAGEMENT STRUCTURE

Organization and management are the legal structure of your business, which determines which type of income tax return form you have to file, as you do have to pay Uncle Sam. The most common forms of businesses are a sole proprietorship, partnership (LLC), corporation, or S-corporation. If your venture involves your teaming up with others, you might want to provide some information about what makes your team special, such as team members' portfolios, resumes, awards, certifications, and anything else that makes them shine bright like a diamond.

SERVICE OR PRODUCT

What products or services are you offering to the world marketplace? As I mentioned earlier, the marketplace is looking for what is in you and what you have to offer. You need to explain this offer and how it benefits your prospects or potential clients. You should also ensure your work or your brand is protected, so consider copyright or patent filings.

MARKETING AND SALES PLAN

This is where you describe how you will market your business. You'll share your sales strategy and detail how you will make the sales.

FUNDING REQUEST

Last but not least, you talk about your funding request. This is where you create and calculate projections.

For you to forecast your financial projections for your business, you've got to use foresight, or what I like to call four-sight or four eyes—two eyes to see the past and present and another two to see into the future.

You have the choice of either raising capital yourself or looking for an investor to invest in your product, service, or business. In the several cases of monetization you reviewed, I mentioned how Mikaila and Mo were on *Shark Tank*. They were pitching their product or business to the "sharks," who served as their investors. If the shark was sold on a pitch, they purchased a percentage of the presenter's company and provided them with the funding and operational costs they needed to jumpstart or grow their businesses.

If you plan to fundraise, list in this section how much money you'll need for the next three to five years. You need to clearly explain what you will use the funds for. For example, you might want to allocate funds toward specific equipment, materials, bills, and monies to pay your team's (employees') salaries until you raise additional capital to pay for it from income. This financial investment can get you from walking to running to a business that's booming.

Activity

**Magic Makers
It's all in the details**

ACTIVITY

MAGIC MAKERS
IT'S ALL IN THE DETAILS

IN THIS ACTIVITY, YOU ARE GOING TO CREATE YOUR BUSINESS PLAN. AS YOU CREATE, REMEMBER THE WORDS OF WALT DISNEY, "THERE IS NO MAGIC IN MAGIC. IT'S ALL IN THE DETAILS." DO YOUR BEST TO BE VERY SPECIFIC, CLEAR, AND DETAILED. I BELIEVE WE ARE SET FOR TAKEOFF…

What is your executive summary?

____
____
____
____
____
____

What is your company description?

Your mission statement

____
____
____
____

____

____

What problem does your product, service, or offer solve?

____

____

____

____

____

What demographic, or whom, do you plan to serve? Be specific!

____

____

____

____

____

What is your market analysis?

____

____

____

____

____

List at least three of your competitors in your related industry.

____

____

____

____

Identify three strengths and weaknesses of each competitor.

Competitor Name	Strengths	Weakness

How can you do what they do better and distinguish yourself from the rest of the pack? Share what makes your offer so unique.

____

____

____

____

____

What is the organizational and management structure for your business?

____

____

____

____

____

I ISSUE A CHALLENGE HERE TO YOU: RESEARCH THE MOST COMMON LEGAL FORMS TO A BUSINESS, SUCH AS SOLE PROPRIETORSHIP, PARTNERSHIP (LLC), CORPORATION, AND C- OR S-CORPORATION, TO FIND YOUR FIT.

Define each of the following legal business structures and, based on your research, identify what tax advantage it might have for your business.

Sole Proprietorship

____
____
____
____
____
____

Limited Liability Company (LLC)

____
____
____
____
____
____

C- and S-Corporation

____
____
____
____
____
____

What is your service or product?

____
____
____

____

____

____

What is your marketing and sales plan?

____

____

____

____

____

If you have a funding request, how much money will you need to cover expenses for the next three to five years?

____

____

____

____

____

What is the purpose of the funds? How will you use them?

____

____

____

____

____

____

BONUS QUESTION

How could you fundraise for your business?

____

____

____

____

____

____

Notes

[1] "Write your business plan," U.S. Small Business Association, accessed July 3, 2019, https://www.sba.gov/business-guide/plan-your-business/write-your-business-plan.

A Final Word

Live Full, Expire Empty

CHAPTER 8

A Final Word
Live Full, Expire Empty

I believe

The two greatest tragedies in life are to live with no purpose and to die with potential.

Potential is untapped power and unused ability. It is the strength in you that lies dormant, everything you can be but have not yet become. It is never what you've done but rather what you can do but have not yet done. It is always measured in how far you could go but have not gone.

As our journey together comes to a close, I encourage you to find yourself in order to lose yourself to a cause that is bigger and greater than you. Let it be said of you that you lived full and expired empty, refusing to settle for a life less than the one you are capable of living, and that you have been intentional in seeking to develop and master the ability that is in you.

I wrote in previous chapters that the marketplace of the world is looking for what you have to offer. If you can locate your abilities and harness them, I offer to you that you can find your place in the world, not just to be profitable but to be purposeful and impactful.

I leave you to mediate and mull over these questions. Would you make it a point that these essential questions do not go unanswered?

Who am I?

Why am I here?

What can I do?

Where am I going?

Acknowledgments

To my family, your love and sacrifice for me has never gone unnoticed.

To my love, I build for you and our future generations.

To my friends and mentors, you have held me up when I did not have the strength to stand and you have shown me the way when my eyes failed me.

To those I inspire, look to me as only an example of what is beyond possible for you.

About the Author

Jeffrey Ulysse, M.S.Ed. is a Brooklyn-born financial literacy coach, international empowerment speaker, entrepreneur, and author. He is the CEO of JU Consultants, an educational consulting company that provides socio-emotional programs and financial education to youth, parents, and families. In addition, he is the cofounder of Alchemic Solutions, a program designed to teach young men of color emotional intelligence and equip them with transactional language.

As one who has been invited to speak around the globe, Mr Ulysse has an unapologetic passion for youth and young adults and has committed his life to the socio-emotional, emotional, and financial development of our youth. Mr Ulysse lives to give and believes we can create the lives we've imagined.

Connect with Jeffrey

If you would like to stay connected with Jeffrey Ulysse, feel free to follow on Instagram and LinkedIn.

WEBSITE: www.juconsultants.com
currently building a new website: www.jeffreyulysse.com

EMAIL: info@juconsultants.com

INSTAGRAM: @jeffreyulysse

LINKEDIN: @jeffreyulysse

All About My Money

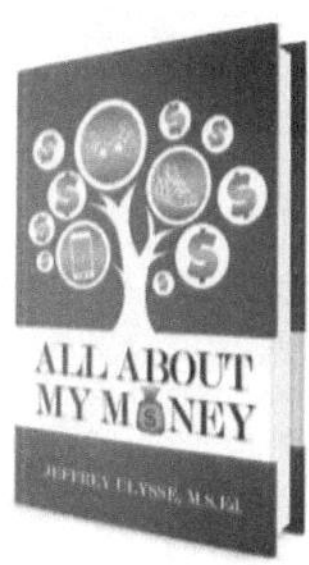

All About My Money is a guide designed to teach youth and young adults on how to build, manage, and sustain wealth and the importance of getting into a relationship with their money.

In this book you will learn,

1. how to turn your passion into profit,
2. the 7 ways to becoming financially fit,
3. how to save now, so you can turn up later,
4. why poor planning leads to poor pockets, and
5. how to plant your money tree.

Order From

AMAZON: https://www.amazon.com/All-About-Money-Jeffrey-Ulysse/dp/0692144137